Communities Bounty
by Rachel Winton

To my family, friends, and community, thanks for the inspiration that fuels my creativity.

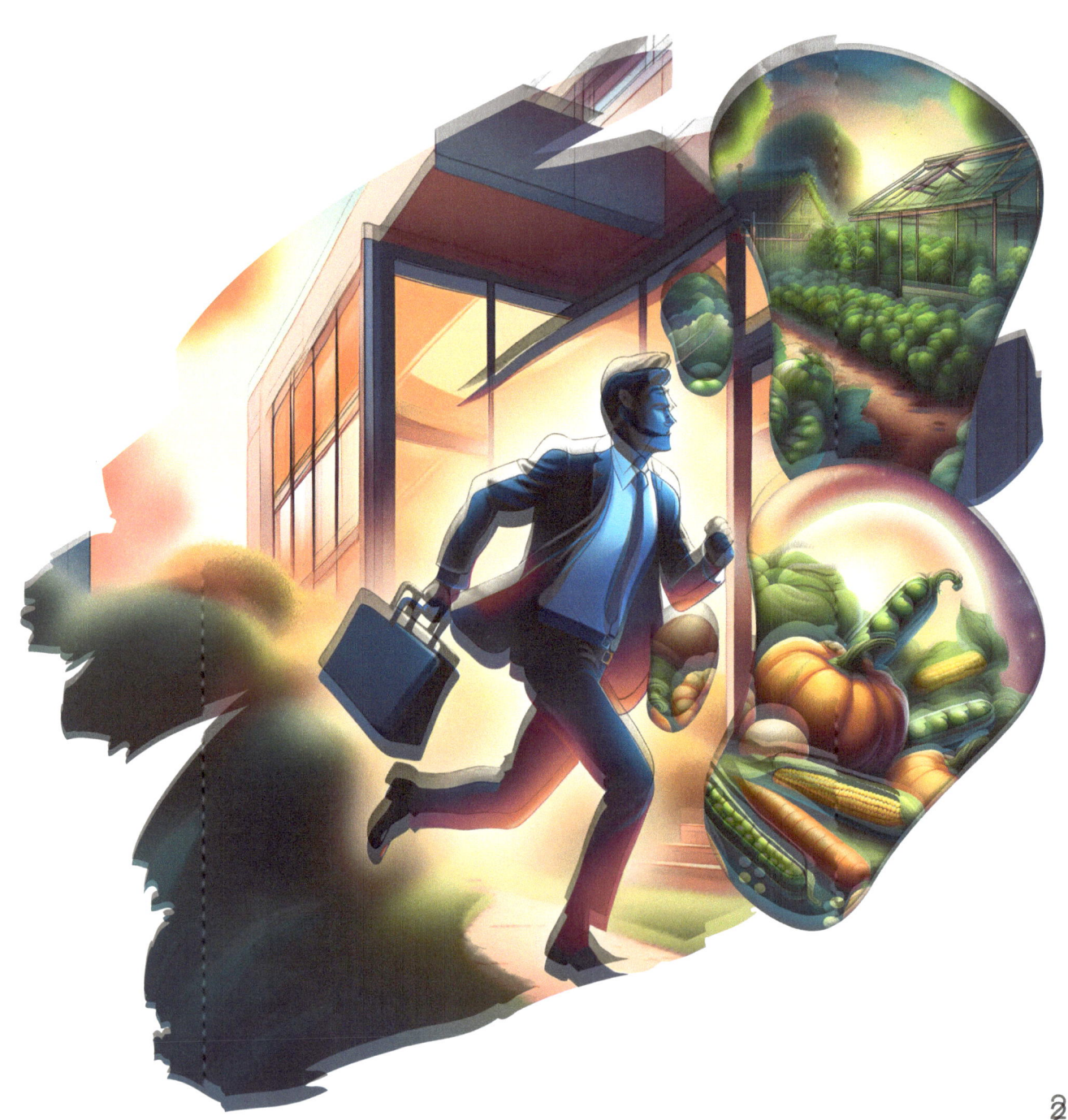

Through hasty veils, we seek a trail unseen,
where roots intertwine, weaving a fertile dream.
By placing hands in earth, our spirits unwind,
to feed the future sustainably, our woes unbind.

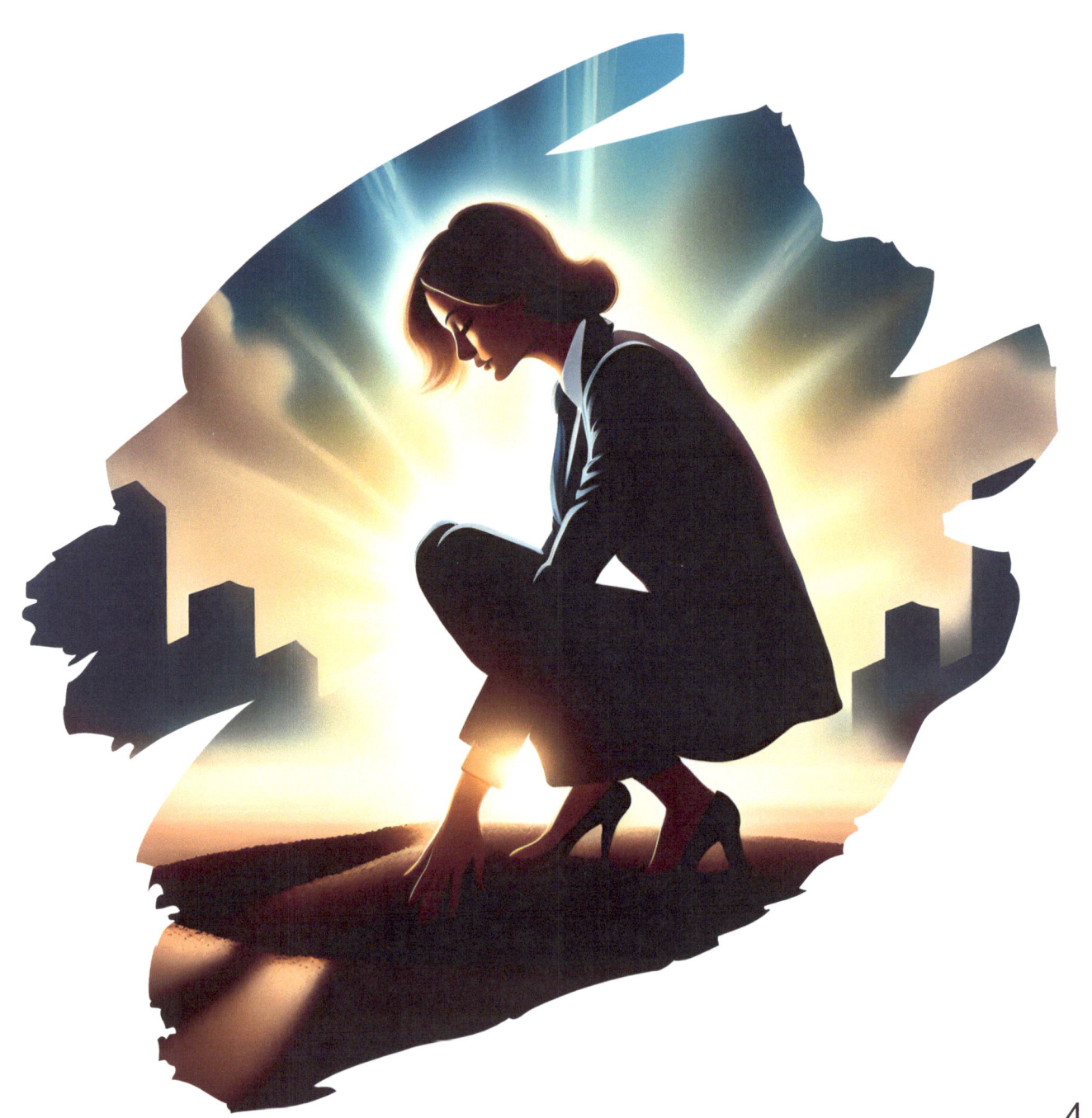

Early to the garden we soar, our joy renewed by feeling the breeze.
In a symphony of whispers, the sight of endless opportunities please.
Beneath the boundless heavens, our imagination takes flight.
We wander, we envision, and reach for celestial light.

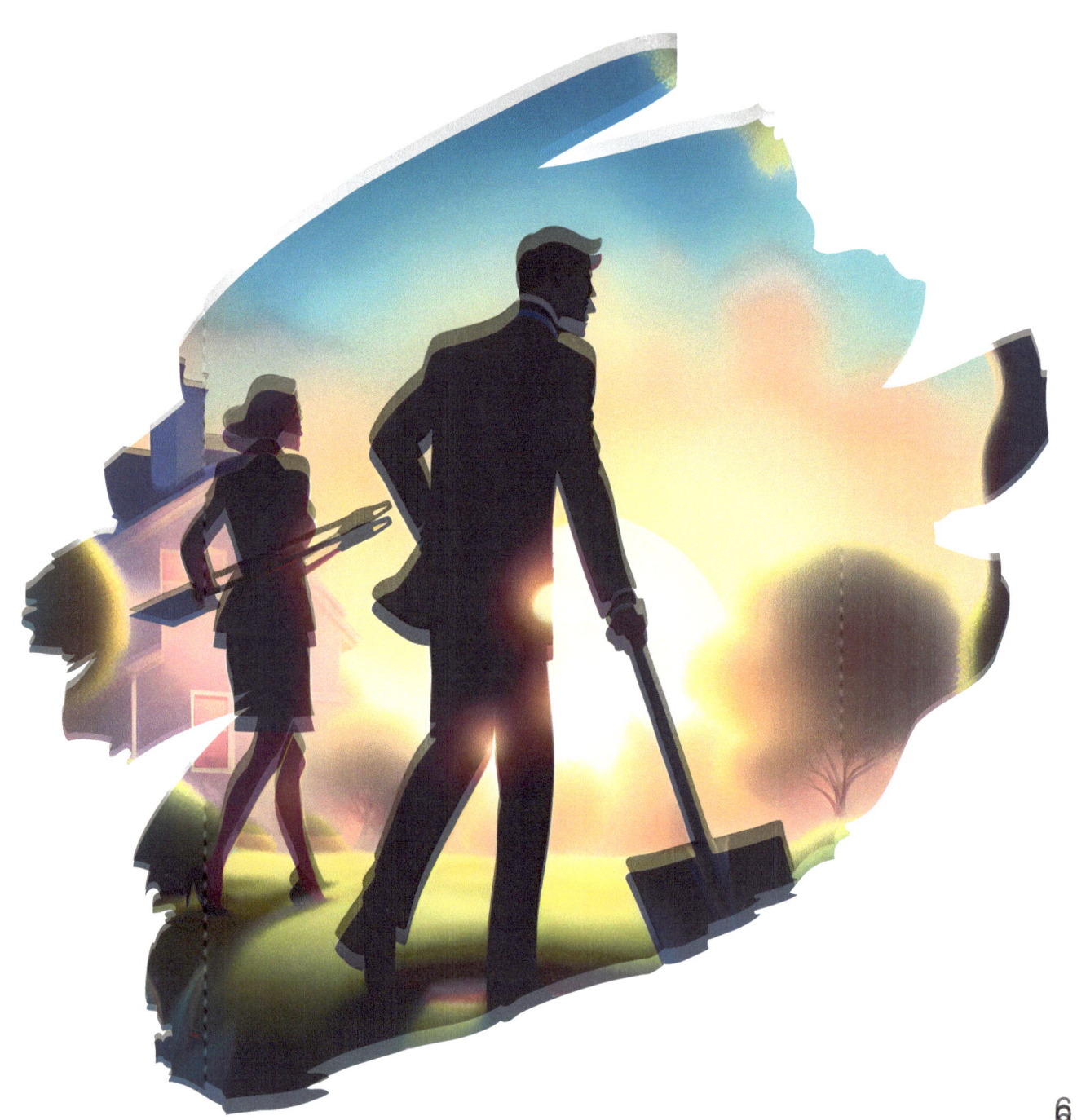

At daybreak, our steps grace the lands
moistened visage.
All eager to plant, in nature's sacred carriage.
Planning to sow seeds of promise in spring's
rich earth, we unite,
in a dance of endurance and rebirth, we'll toil
easing our plight.

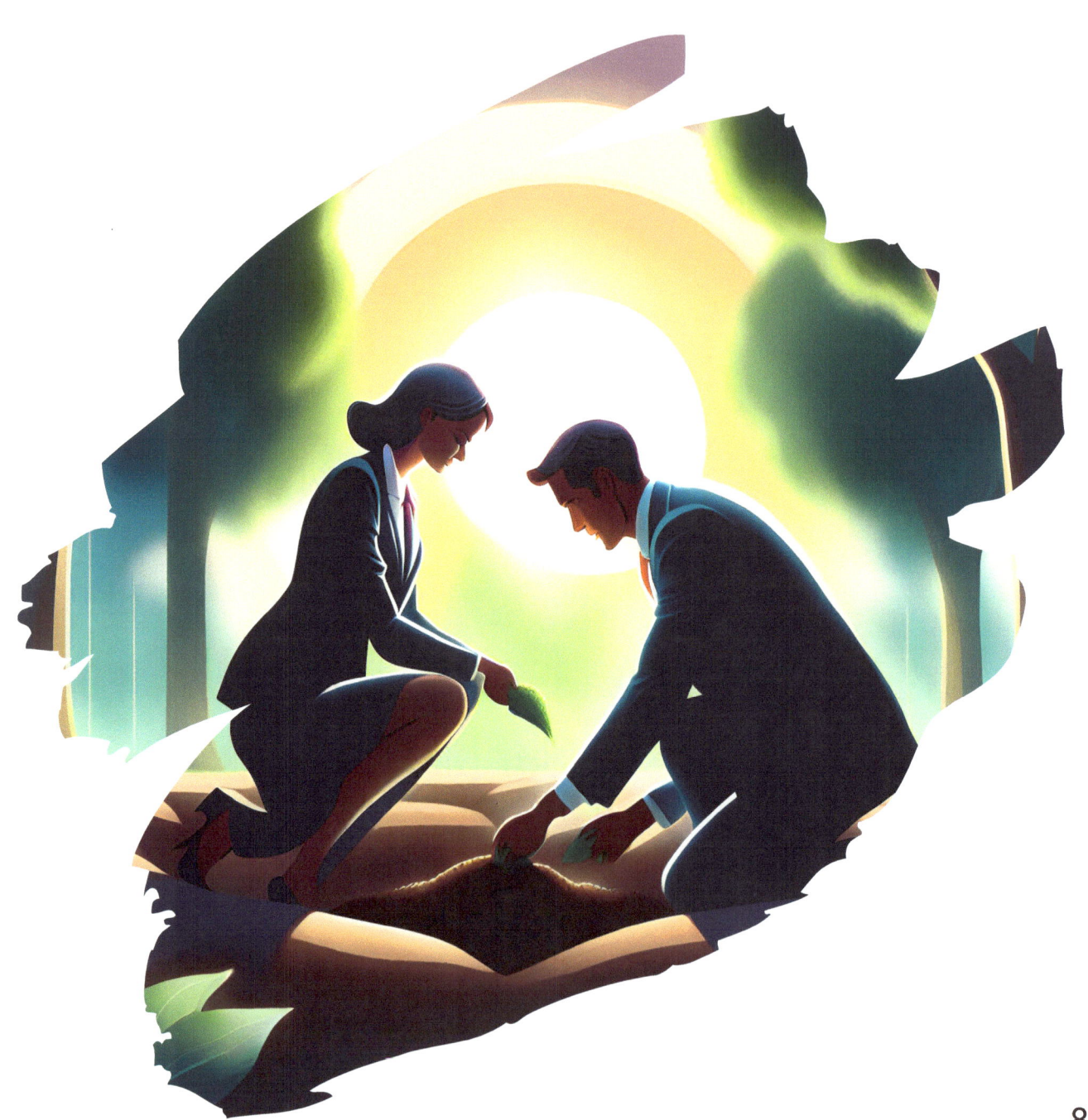

Within the tender embrace of earth, our fingers connect,
weaving snug cradles for seeds and seedlings, both to protect.
With care we nurture, as aspirations soar and align,
sowing a plume of dreams for tomorrows bountiful shrine.

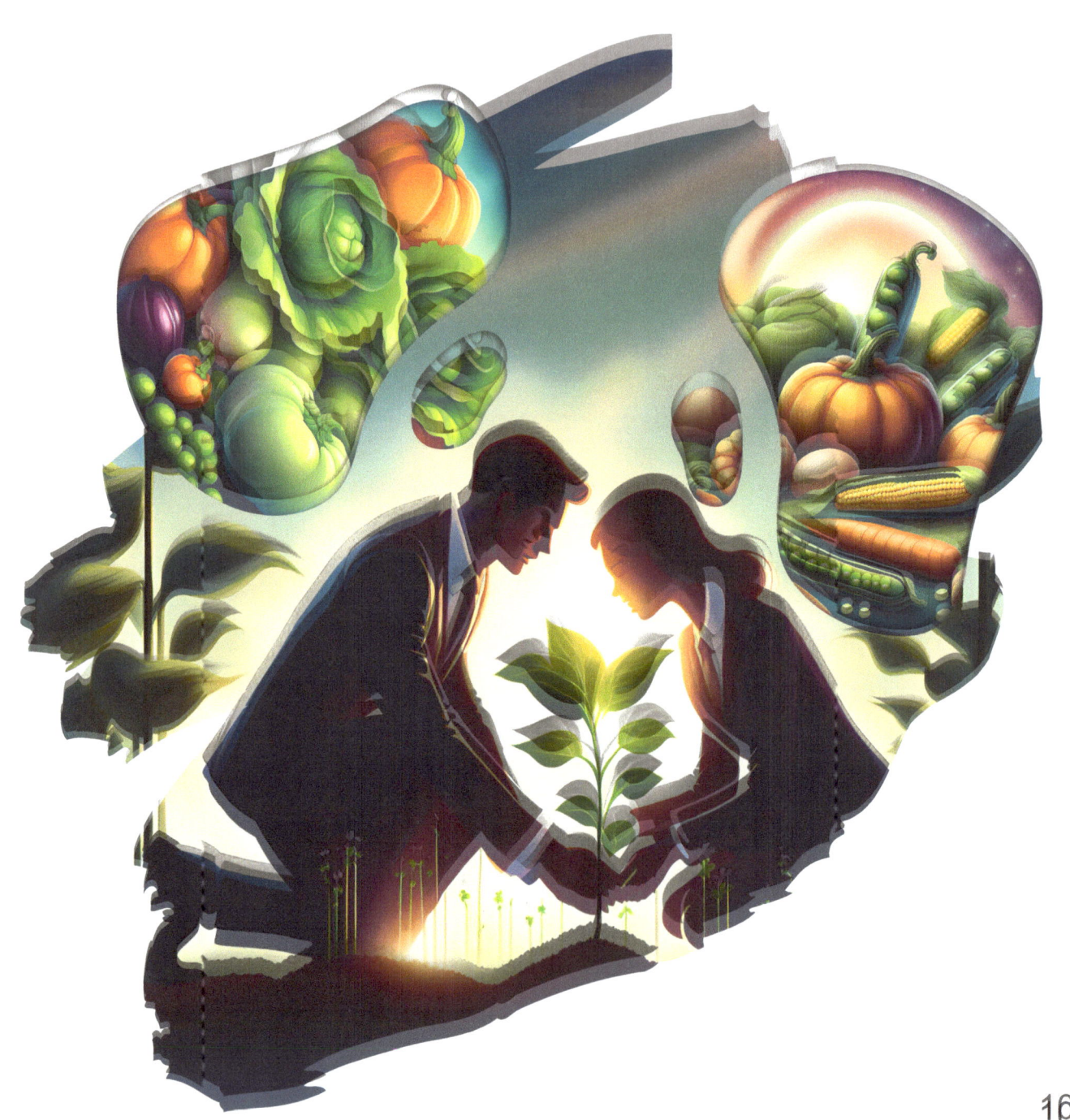

In the gentle hug of spring's embrace,
seeds in hand, a green dream we chase.
Lettuce, pumpkin, peas, beans, and carrots unite,
Prepare for a future dance under the sun's bright light:

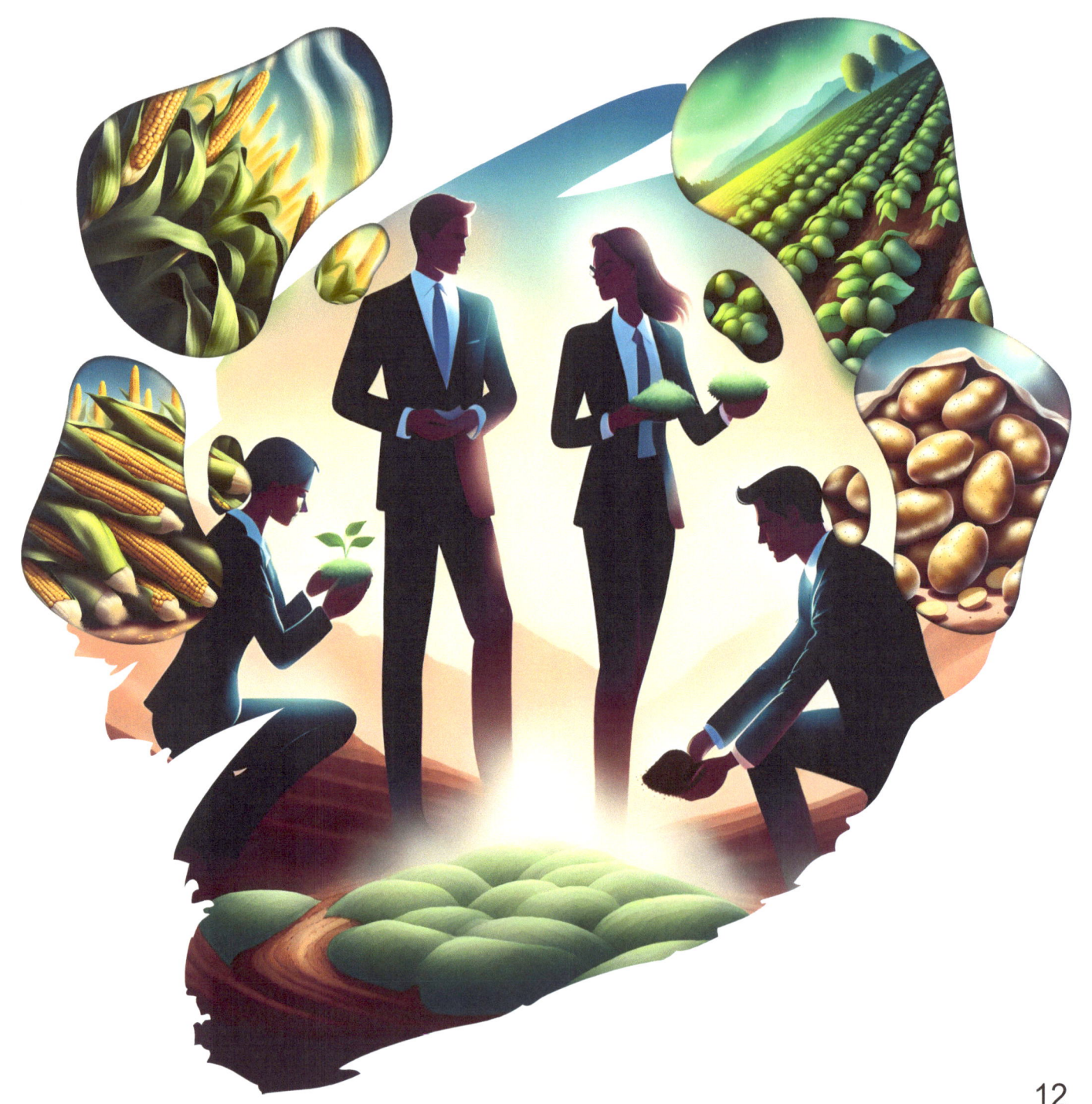

Our souls shall continue the journey, never to compromise,
planting corn to hear the wind's secrets, and potatoes with their all seeing eyes.
Every root and seed, a tribute to fortitude and nurturing grace.
Upholding communities, this sacred journey we embrace.

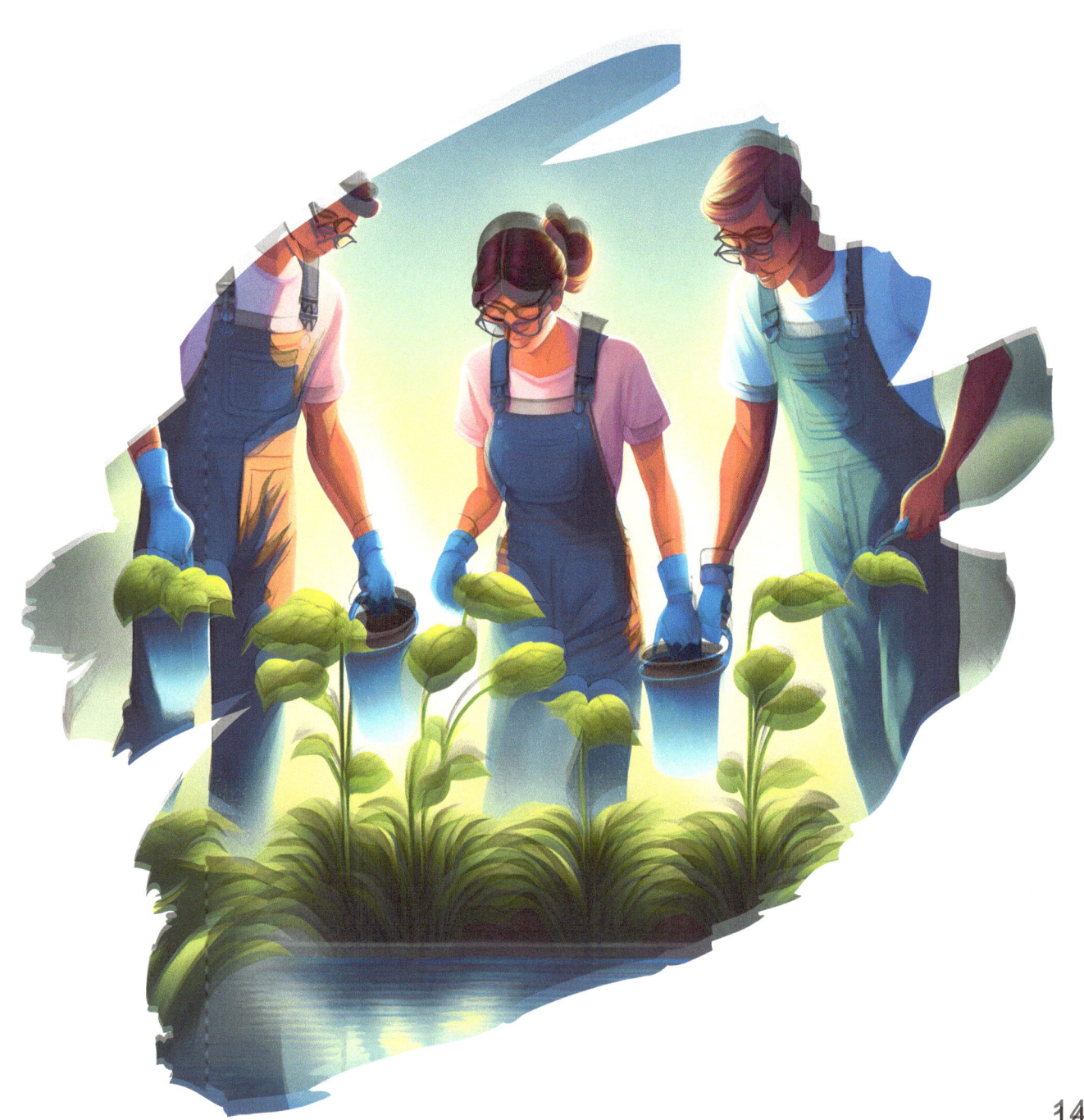

With a sprinkle of water, we pamper freshly planted seeds.
A cozy mulch cover, gently tucked in, secures their needs.
Through this ritual, we forge strength, a tribute to our determination,
Easing our way in the dance of nature's transformation.

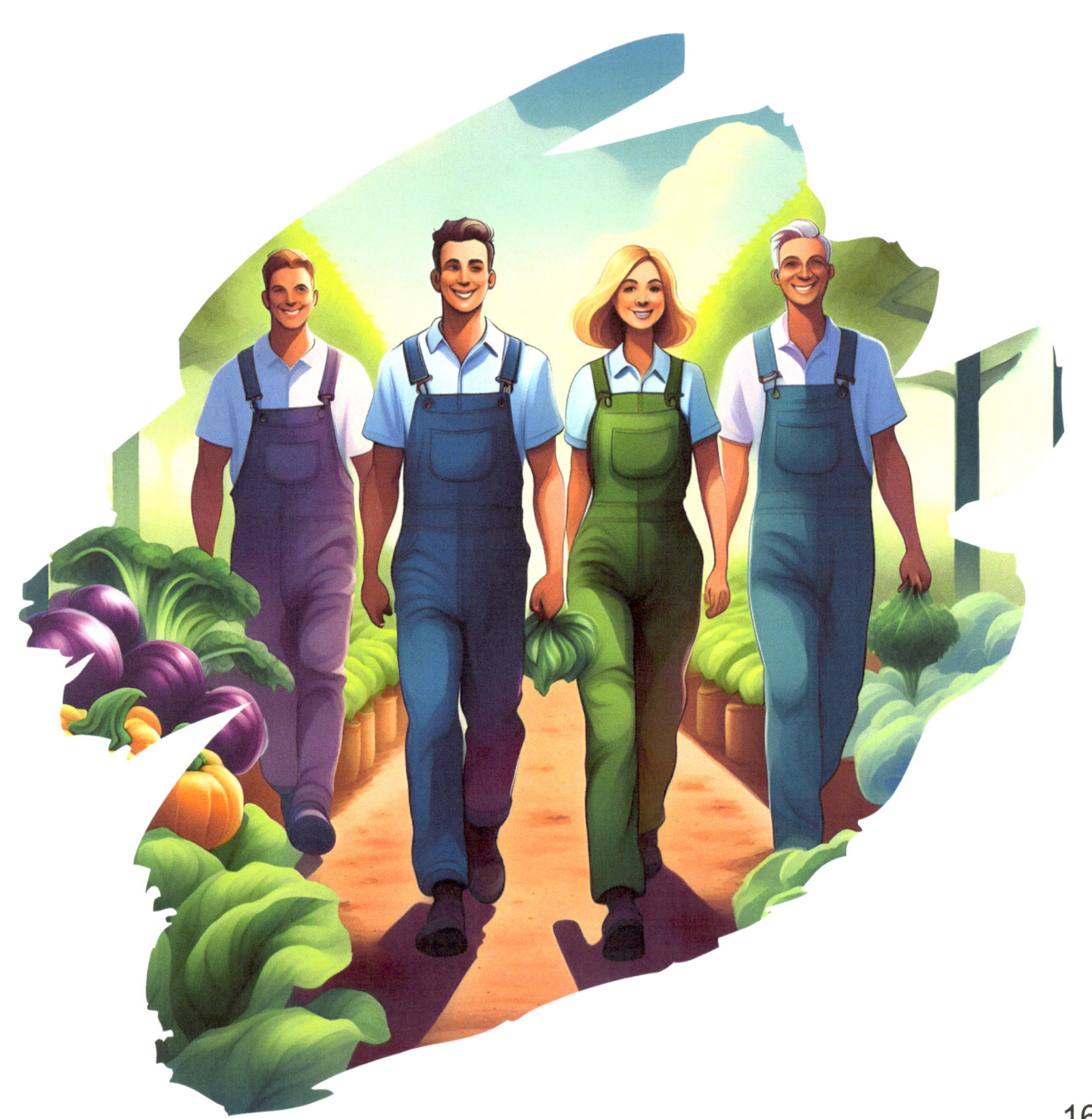

In our garden's lively, buzzing mix,
We make sure to pair flowers with veggies, in a sight that just clicks.
To draw in pollinators and wave pests goodbye,
They will flourish together, under the endless sky.

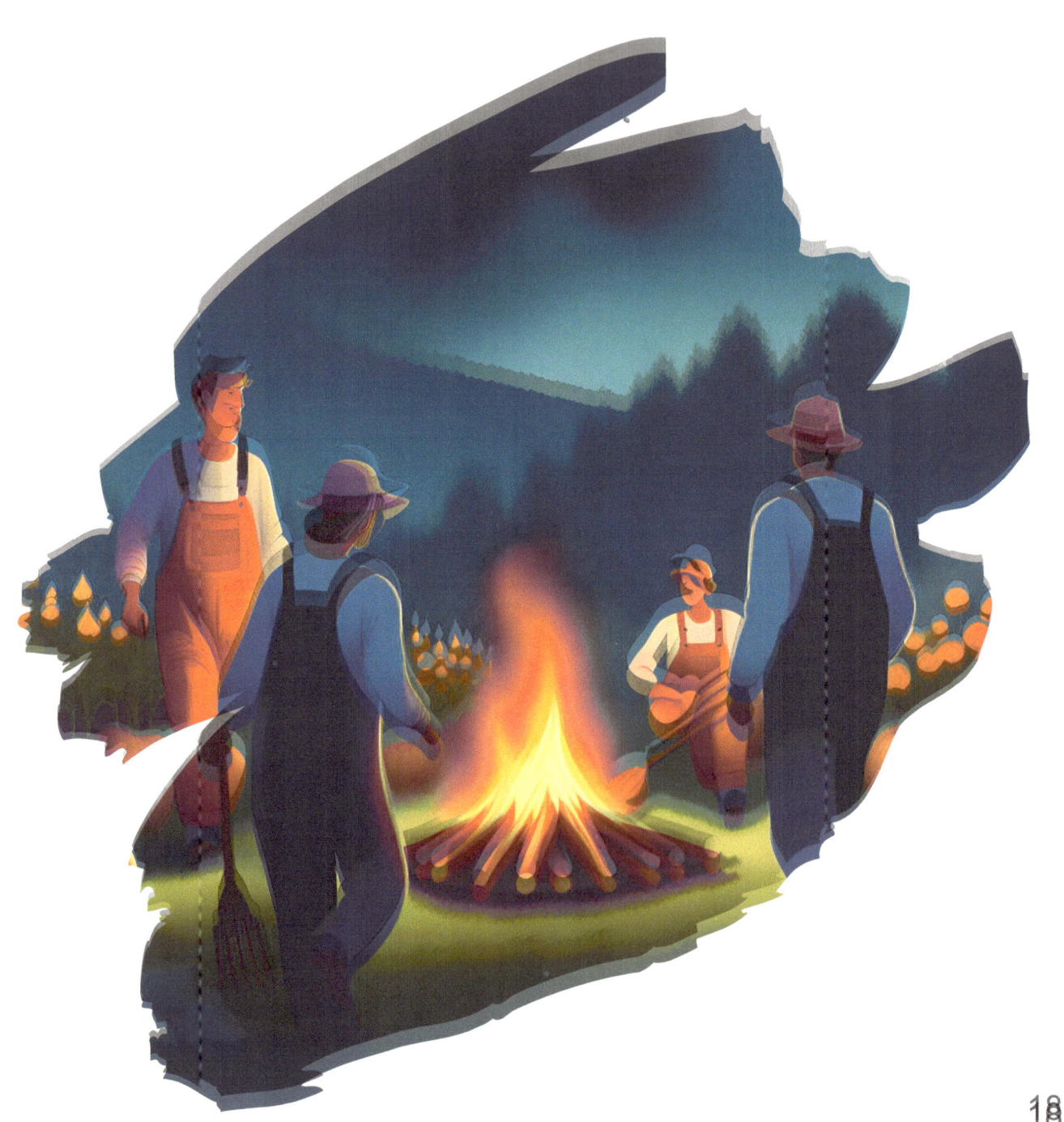

Beneath the darkening sky, as labour wanes,
homeward bound we stride and dream of future gains.
Around the hearth, mirth dances in a timeless blend.
Embraced by friends, family and community,
in feasts shared, souls on the mend.

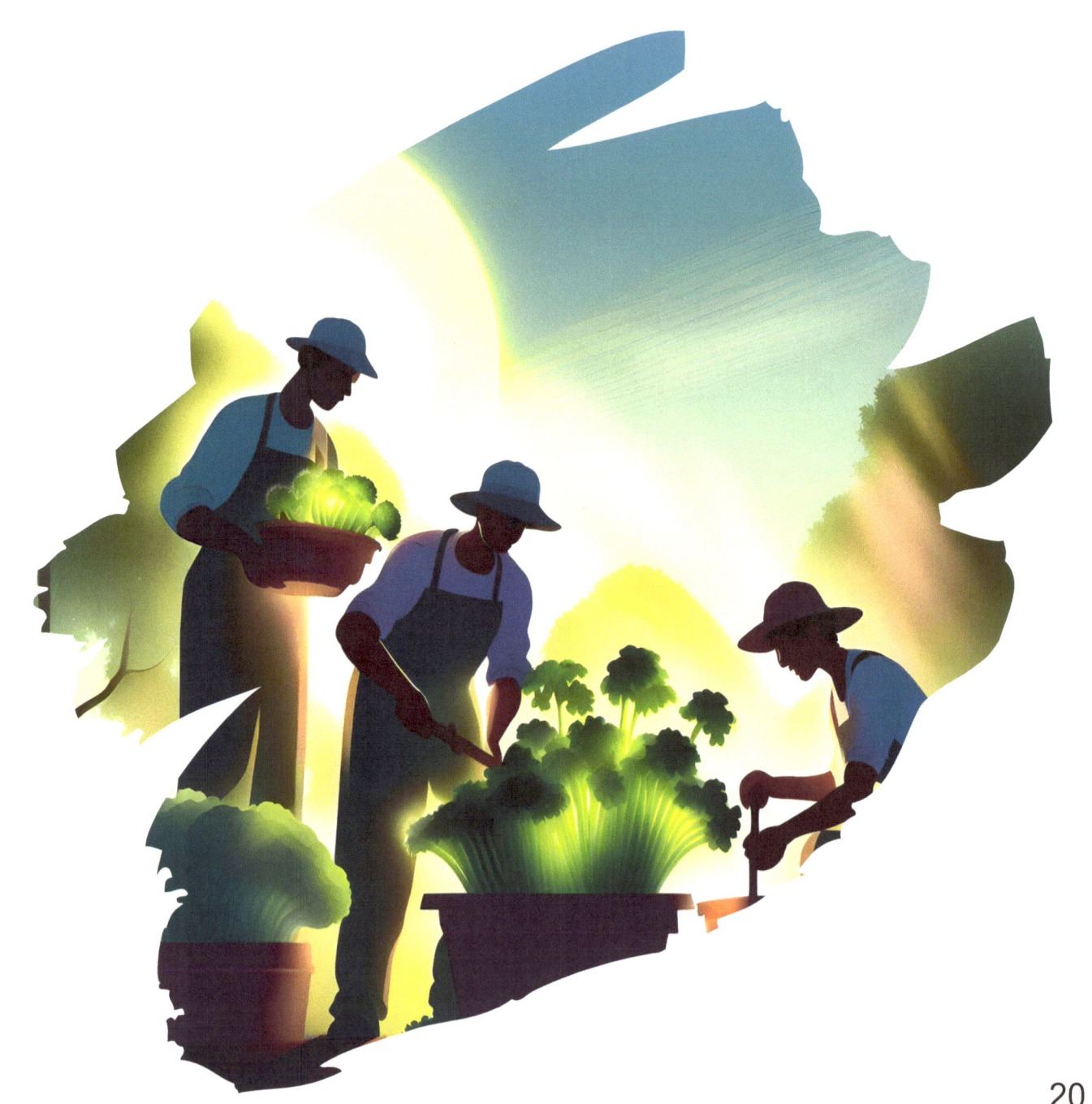

When harvest calls, we'll choose with care.
Vegetables fresh, from land to plate, a fare.
For health, for Earth, our choices keen,
Sustaining us, and the planet green.

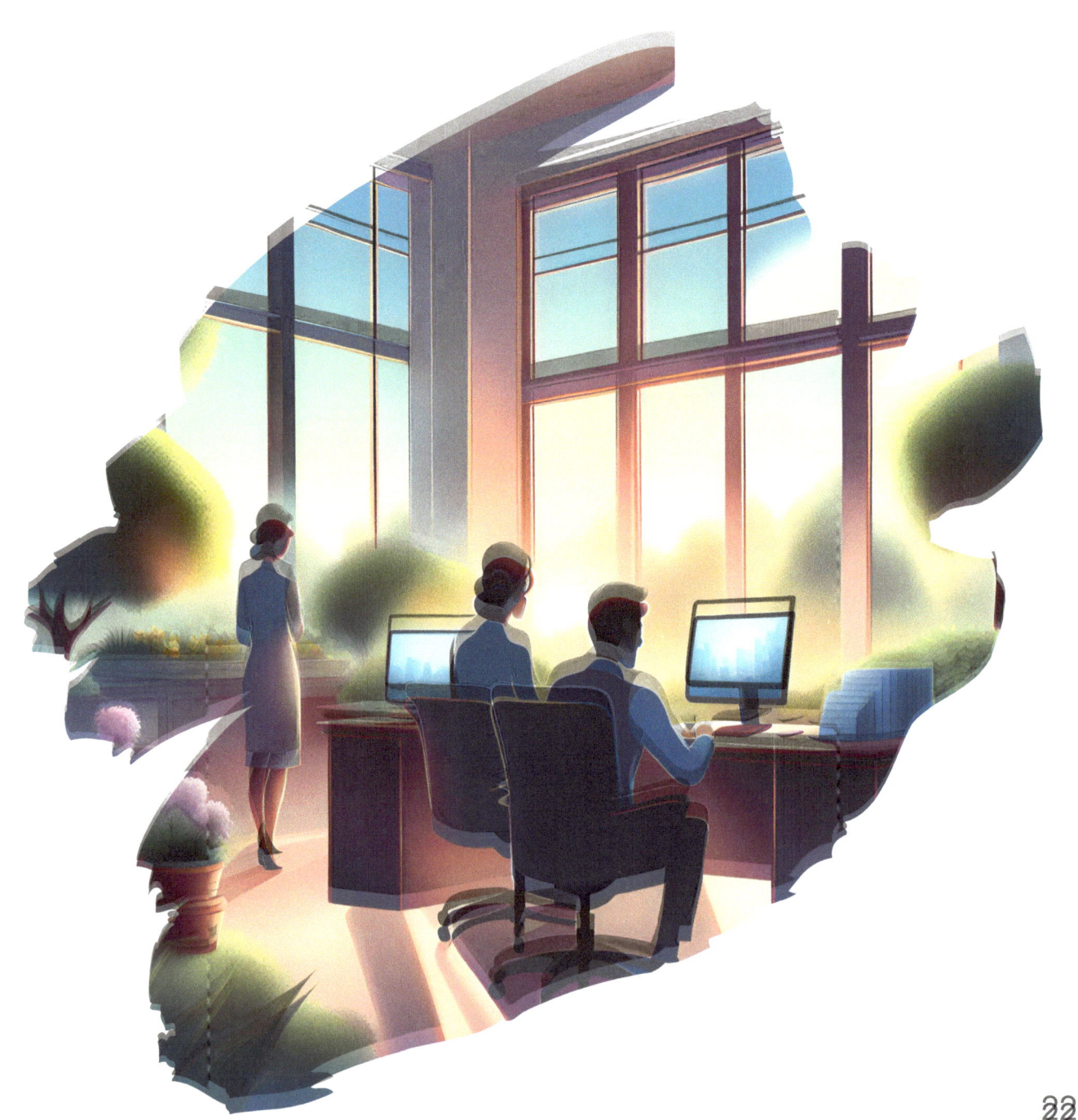

We bartered seeds for screens, forsaking
nature's cradle in our haste.
Chasing ephemeral dreams, leaving gardens
in our wake, overgrown, misplaced.
But in each tender shoot, a steadfast plea to
endure and remain,
Our roots whisper wisdom, for genuine growth
is never in vain.

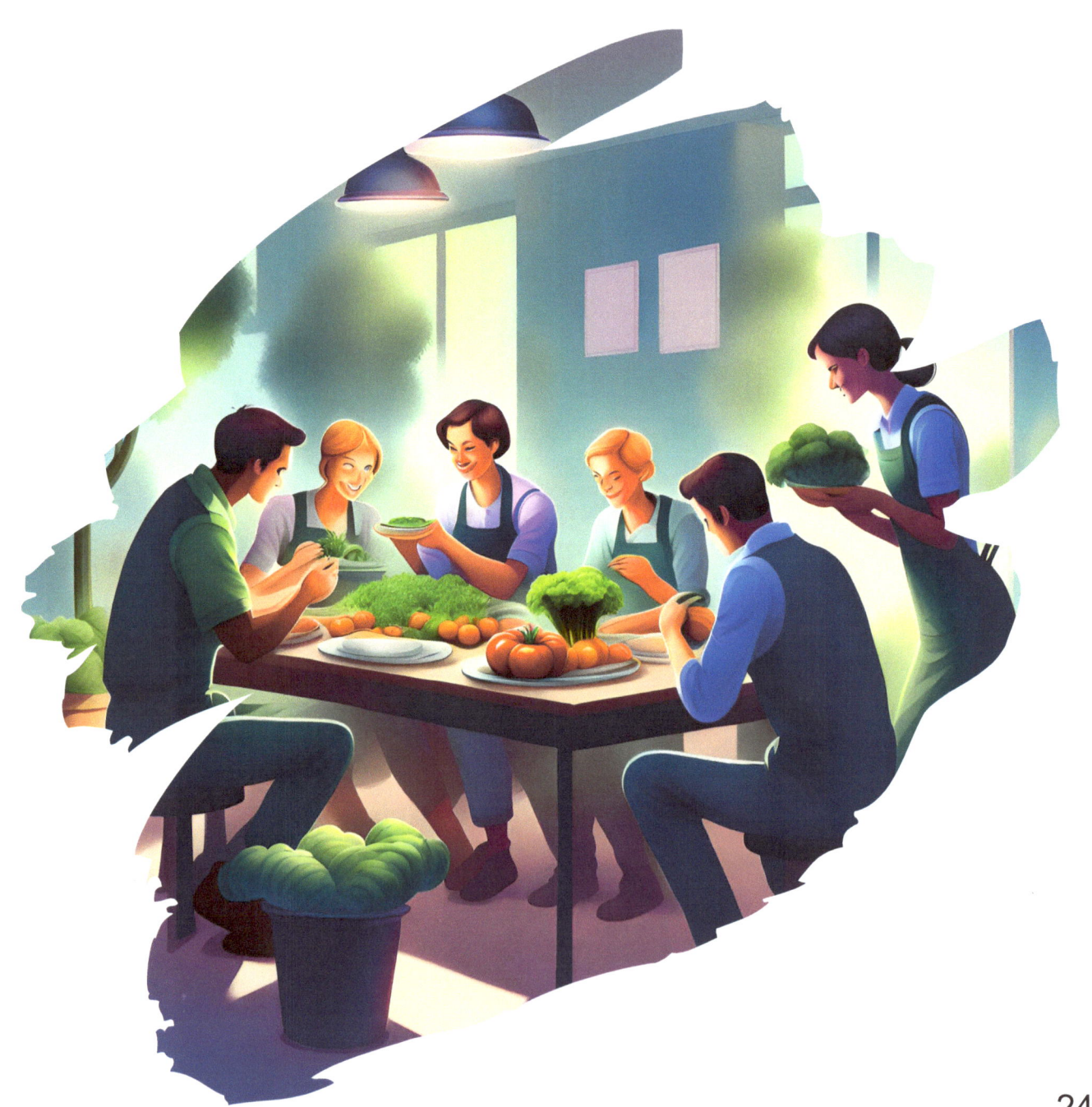

www.ingramcontent.com/pod-product-compliance
Lightning Source LLC
Chambersburg PA
CBHW051951210526
45473CB00020B/2370